4/15

RHYMING POEMS

BY LISA M. BOLT SIMONS

ILLUSTRATED BY KATHLEEN PETELINSEK

The Child's World®

Published by The Child's World®
1980 Lookout Drive · Mankato, MN 56003-1705
800-599-READ · www.childsworld.com

ACKNOWLEDGMENTS
The Child's World®: Mary Berendes, Publishing Director
Red Line Editorial: Editorial direction
The Design Lab: Design and production

Photographs ©: Photodisc/Thinkstock, 6; Getty Images
Entertainment/Thinkstock, 13; iStock/Thinkstock, 19

ISBN 9781631436987
LCCN 2014945395

Printed in the United States of America
Mankato, MN
November, 2014
PA02240

About the Author

Lisa M. Bolt Simons is a writer
and a teacher. She has published
more than ten books for children.
She has also been awarded grants
and awards for her writing. Besides
writing, teaching has been her
passion for 20 years. She lives in
Minnesota with her husband and
boy/girl twin teenagers. Her Web site
is *www.lisamboltsimons.com*.

About the Illustrator

Kathleen Petelinsek is a graphic
designer and illustrator. She has been
designing and illustrating books for
children for 20 years. She lives in
Minnesota with her husband, two
dogs, a cat, and three fancy chickens.

TABLE OF CONTENTS

What Is Poetry?

Do you know how old poetry is? People have been writing poems for more than 3,000 years! Before words were written on paper, people shared poetry orally. That means it was spoken. Most poetry is written now. There are many styles and lengths of poems. Some poetry is the length of an adult book. Other poems are only a few lines long.

There are a lot of special things that make poetry different than other writing. One is that poems often use lines instead of sentences. A line can be a long phrase. It can also be a single word. A line doesn't have to be a complete thought.

Poems also have rhythm. This is the way the words in a poem sound together. Rhythm is created from the **syllables** in a poem. These are the different sound parts that make up a word. For example, *zoo* has only one syllable. *Cir-cus* has two syllables. The way words are spoken also affects the rhythm. A syllable can be **stressed** or unstressed. The first syllable of *CIR-cus* is stressed. This means our voice is stronger when we say that syllable.

Poems with rhymes often sound like songs. Many poems are turned into songs. Lyrics are poems that go with music.

Another important part of poetry is the sound of the words. Sometimes the sound includes words that rhyme. Two words rhyme when their last syllables sound the same. But not all poems rhyme. Poetic sound sometimes comes from repeated words or lines. It also comes from the poem's rhythm.

Poetry often creates images, or pictures, inside readers' heads. Strong, descriptive words help create images. Sometimes a reader must **infer**, or guess, what the poem is about. A reader can use images to figure out what's happening in a poem. Other times a poet states exactly what he or she means.

WHAT IS A RHYMING POEM?

A rhyming poem is just that—a poem in which the ends of lines rhyme. Rhyming originally came from the Arabic language. Rhymes became more common in European poems starting in the 1100s. Today, a lot of poems rhyme!

There are many different types of rhymes. Let's learn more about the different ways you can write a rhyming poem.

Paper **Ink**

Oh, look!
It's a book
made of paper and ink.
I feel giddy, I think,
but don't mean to be smug—
a book needs no plug.

?

What words rhyme in this poem?

Different Kinds of Rhymes

Rhyme is about sound, not spelling. *Bat* and *cat* rhyme. But *dirt* and *hurt* also rhyme. The English language has a lot of spelling rules. Words that look different may still sound the same. For example, listen to the *F* sound in *tough* and *puff*. They are the same sound. But they do not use the same letters. Since the *F*'s sound the same, the words still rhyme.

Poems have many different kinds of rhymes. True rhymes are the first rhymes poets learn in school. They are

bat

cat

habitat

placemat

key

knee

easy

cavity

heard most often in nursery rhymes and songs. True rhymes have the same **vowel** sound. They also have the same **consonant** end sound. *Bat*, *cat*, *placemat*, and *habitat* are known as true rhymes. What about *see*, *key*, *knee*, *easy*, and *cavity*? Those words aren't all spelled the same. But they have the same end sounds. They are also true rhymes.

SLANT RHYMES

A slant rhyme *almost* rhymes. The vowel sounds of words are a bit different. But the consonants at the beginning or end are the same. *Net*, *bat*, and *gut* are slant rhymes. They end in the *T* sound. Let's put them in a poem.

Should you buy a stick, a puck, and **net**?
Or a glove, a ball, and **bat**?
Which sport should you play?
It's not up to me.
You simply go with your **gut**.

Another way to slant rhyme is to have the vowels sound the same. Then the consonants can sound a little different. *Pet* and *bed* are slant rhymes. So are *hug* and *run*.

Dr. Seuss was a famous author who rhymed made-up words. For example, he rhymed "Sneetches" with "beaches" and "wocket" with "pocket."

EYE RHYMES

Eye rhymes are words that look like they should rhyme but don't. They are spelled like they are true rhymes. But their vowel sounds aren't the same. *Love* and *stove* are eye rhymes.

Cookies, cookies
All I love.
Cookies, cookies
I need a stove.

RHYMES CAN BE ANYWHERE!

Rhymes don't have to come at the end of lines. Sometimes the rhymes are in the middle of the line, not at the end. This is called internal rhyme.

"It's easy to see why there's no cavity" has three internal rhymes. *Easy*, *see*, and *cavity* all rhyme with one another.

COLOR CLUES

White is the light every night
that colors the face of the moon.

Lean down, look around for brown,
spot a caterpillar in its cocoon.

A mellow but bright yellow fellow,
the sun is hiding from the stars.

The green in between blossom and dirt
are stems like strings on guitars.

The red on its head and coal-black mask
make a cardinal's handsome face.

Black clouds unpack a cracking attack;
storms boom, pour, and race.

Raindrops bend light with all their might;
spreading color around the world so bright.

?

Which types of rhymes are used in this poem?

CHAPTER THREE

3

Rhyme Schemes

Rhyming poems often have a pattern of rhymes. This is called a rhyme scheme. Rhyme schemes use alphabet letters to represent the end rhymes in lines. Here is the rhyme scheme for the poem in Chapter 1:

Oh, look! **(A)**
It's a book **(A)**
made of paper and ink. **(B)**
I feel giddy, I think, **(B)**
but don't mean to be smug— **(C)**
a book needs no plug. **(C)**

The rhyme scheme would be written like this: *aabbcc*.

There are many different types of rhyme schemes. A **couplet** is a pair of lines that rhymes. A couplet by itself usually has the rhyme scheme *aa*. Couplets can be put together in **stanzas** to create a longer poem. Stanzas are groups of lines. The rhyme scheme is up to the poet. It can vary from *aabbcc* to *ababab* and so on.

Sonnets are one of the most famous forms of rhyming poems. Sonnets have 14 lines. There are many different versions of the sonnet. The rhyme scheme depends on the type of sonnet. William Shakespeare is famous for writing sonnets. He lived in England in the late 1500s.

A tercet has three lines. A quatrain has four lines. Stanzas can have as many lines as a poet wants. Stanzas can be mixed and matched to create longer poems.

Quatrains with four lines are common in rhyming poems. One of the most popular rhyme schemes is *abab*.

THE WEIRD ANIMAL ZOO

The firestick insect is not to fear.
A margay has spots like a jaguar cat
White-striped bongos look like deer;
and a leafy sea dragon—imagine that!

Sifaka lemurs are brown and white.
The mouse-like degu's tail is furry.
The kinkajou is awake all night.
And an okapi's striped legs can run in a hurry.

These odd zoo animals can be quite nice,
some cute, some cuddly, some small.
But Madagascar's aye-aye will
  make you look twice.
It's the weirdest one of them all!

?

What is the rhyme scheme in this poem of quatrains?

NOW IT'S YOUR TURN!

Rhyming poems have been around for thousands of years. By choosing words that rhyme, poets use words in surprising ways. There are many ways to write a rhyming poem. Now that you know more about rhyming poems, it's time to write your own!

TIPS FOR YOUNG POETS

1. Practice makes a good poet. Try writing a new poem every day for a week.

2. Write your poems using strong verbs that create images in readers' heads, like "march" instead of "walk."

3. Make a list of true rhymes. Use this list to write a rhyming poem.

4. Write a couplet with as many internal rhymes as you can.

5. Write a poem about something you like, such as horses, baseball, or summer. Make it serious. Then try to write it again. This time make it funny!

6. Read your poems out loud. Listen closely to how they sound.

7. Don't forget to revise your poems. This means looking at them again and maybe changing some things. Look for boring words you can change to more specific or interesting words.

8. Read books by Dr. Seuss, Shel Silverstein, Marilyn Singer, Jack Prelutsky, and William Shakespeare to learn more about rhyming poetry. Keep an eye out for new poets who write rhyming poems.

GLOSSARY

consonant (KAHN-suh-nuhnt): A consonant is part of the group of letters in the alphabet that are not vowels. The letter *S* is a consonant.

couplet (KUHP-let): A couplet is pair of lines in a poem. In some poems, the two lines of a couplet rhyme.

infer (in-FUR): To infer is to use facts and details to make a good guess about something. When you read a poem, you infer the poet's meaning.

rhyme (RIME): Words that rhyme have the same ending sound. *Tree* and *bee* are words that rhyme.

stanzas (STAN-zuhz): Stanzas are groups of two or more lines in a poem. Stanzas with four lines are called quatrains.

stressed (STREST): A word or syllable is stressed when it is said a bit stronger or louder than another word or syllable. The pattern of stressed and unstressed sounds decides a poem's rhythm.

syllables (SIL-uh-buhlz): Syllables are units of sounds in a word. *Cir-cus* has two syllables.

vowel (VOU-uhl): A vowel is part of the group of five letters of the alphabet that are not consonants. The letter *O* is a vowel.

TO LEARN MORE

BOOKS

Florian, Douglas. *Shiver Me Timbers! Pirate Poems & Paintings*. New York: Beach Land Books, 2012.

Prelutsky, Jack. *Read a Rhyme, Write a Rhyme*. New York: Random House Children's Books, 2009.

Singer, Marilyn. *A Strange Place to Call Home: The World's Most Dangerous Habitats & the Animals That Call Them Home*. San Francisco: Chronicle Books, 2012.

ON THE WEB

Visit our Web site for lots of links about rhyming poems:
www.childsworld.com/links

Note to Parents, Teachers, and Librarians: We routinely check our Web links to make sure they're safe, active sites—so encourage your readers to check them out!

INDEX